# cupcakes
# & cookies

**Women's Weekly**
THE AUSTRALIAN

# CONTENTS

Australian cup and spoon measurements are metric. A conversion chart appears on page 77.

Baking cupcakes and cookies for family and friends not only shows you're thinking of them, it's also an entertaining and imaginative exercise. As crowd-pleasers for parties and events like weddings and teas, or perfect portables for lunchboxes and picnics, these bite-size delights streamline the production process and give vent to your inner artist.

*Pamela Clark*

Food Director

# WHITE CHOCOLATE CAKES
# WITH SEQUIN SWIRLS

**prep + cook time** 50 minutes (+ cooling) **makes** 12

125g butter, chopped coarsely
80g white eating chocolate, chopped coarsely
1 cup (220g) caster sugar
½ cup (125ml) milk
½ cup (75g) plain flour
½ cup (75g) self-raising flour
1 egg
1 tablespoon (edible) sequins
**fluffy frosting**
1 cup (220g) caster sugar
⅓ cup (80ml) water
2 egg whites

**1** Preheat oven to 170°C/150°C fan-forced. Line 12-hole standard muffin pan with paper cases.
**2** Stir butter, chocolate, sugar and milk in small saucepan over low heat until smooth. Transfer mixture to medium bowl; cool 15 minutes.
**3** Whisk sifted flours into chocolate mixture, then egg. Drop ¼ cup of mixture into cases.
**4** Bake cakes about 30 minutes. Stand in pan 5 minutes; turn, top-side up, onto wire rack to cool.
**5** Meanwhile, make fluffy frosting.
**6** Place frosting into large piping bag fitted with a large fluted tube. Pipe a swirl onto each cake; sprinkle with edible sequins.

**fluffy frosting** Stir sugar and the water in small saucepan over heat, without boiling, until sugar is dissolved. Boil, uncovered, without stirring, 5 minutes or until syrup reaches 116°C on a candy thermometer. Syrup should be thick but not coloured. Remove from heat, allow bubbles to subside. Beat egg whites in small bowl with electric mixer until soft peaks form. While motor is operating, add hot syrup in a thin stream; beat on high speed 10 minutes or until thick.

**tip** If you don't have a candy thermometer, boil the syrup until it's thick with heavy bubbles. Remove from heat, let bubbles subside, then assess the thickness of the syrup.

CUPCAKES

gluten-free chocolate cupcakes

## FROU FROU

prep + cook time **1 hour** makes **12**

125g butter, softened
1 cup (220g) caster sugar
3 eggs
½ cup (75g) plain flour
¼ cup (35g) self-raising flour
½ cup (40g) desiccated coconut
⅓ cup (80g) sour cream
150g frozen raspberries
1 cup (50g) flaked coconut, toasted
15 fresh raspberries, extra, halved
cream cheese frosting
60g butter, softened
160g cream cheese, softened
2 teaspoons coconut essence
3 cups (480g) icing sugar

**1** Preheat oven to 180°C/160°C fan-forced. Line 12-hole standard muffin pan with paper cases.
**2** Beat butter, sugar and eggs in small bowl with electric mixer until light and fluffy. Stir in sifted flours, desiccated coconut, cream and frozen raspberries. Divide mixture into cases; smooth surface.
**3** Bake cakes about 40 minutes. Turn cakes onto wire rack to cool.
**4** Make cream cheese frosting.
**5** Remove cases from cakes; cover with frosting. Decorate with flaked coconut and raspberries.
**cream cheese frosting** Beat butter, cream cheese and essence in small bowl with electric mixer until light and fluffy; gradually beat in sifted icing sugar.

## GLUTEN-FREE CHOCOLATE CUPCAKES

prep + cook time **1 hour 10 minutes (+ cooling & refrigeration)** makes **12**

125g dairy-free spread
100g dark eating chocolate (70% cocoa solids), chopped coarsely
¾ cup (180ml) gluten-free soy milk
¾ cup (165g) caster sugar
1 cup (135g) gluten-free self-raising flour
½ cup (70g) gluten-free plain flour
2 tablespoons cocoa powder

frou frou

fudge frosting
¼ cup (55g) caster sugar
50g dairy-free spread
2 tablespoons water
¾ cup (120g) pure icing sugar
2 tablespoons cocoa powder

**1** Preheat oven to 150°C/130°C fan-forced. Line 12-hole standard muffin pan with paper cases.
**2** Stir spread, chocolate, milk and sugar in medium saucepan over low heat until smooth. Transfer mixture to large bowl; cool 10 minutes.
**3** Whisk sifted flours and cocoa into chocolate mixture until smooth. Divide into paper cases.
**4** Bake cakes 35 minutes. Stand 10 minutes; turn, top-side up, onto wire rack to cool.
**5** Meanwhile, make fudge frosting.
**6** Using 2cm fluted tube, pipe fudge frosting onto cold cakes.
**fudge frosting** Stir caster sugar, spread and the water in small saucepan over low heat until sugar dissolves. Combine sifted icing sugar and cocoa in small bowl; gradually stir in hot sugar mixture until smooth. Cover; refrigerate 20 minutes. Beat frosting until spreadable.

coffee caramel cakes

## COFFEE CARAMEL CAKES

prep + cook time **35 minutes** makes **12**

125g butter, softened
⅔ cup (150g) firmly packed brown sugar
2 tablespoons ground coffee
1 tablespoon boiling water
2 eggs
2 cups (300g) self-raising flour
½ cup (125ml) milk
18 jersey caramels, halved
1 tablespoon icing sugar

**1** Preheat oven to 180°C/160°C fan-forced. Line 12-hole standard muffin pan with paper cases.
**2** Beat butter and sugar in small bowl with electric mixer until light and fluffy. Add combined coffee and water, then beat in eggs, one at a time, beating until just combined between additions. Transfer mixture to large bowl.
**3** Stir in sifted flour and milk. Divide mixture among cases. Press 3 caramel halves into the centre of each cake; cover with batter.
**4** Bake 20 minutes or until browned. Stand in pan 5 minutes; turn, top-side up, onto wire rack to cool. Serve dusted with sifted icing sugar.

## HUMMINGBIRD CAKES WITH COCONUT CRUST

prep + cook time **45 minutes** makes **18**

440g can crushed pineapple in syrup
1 cup (150g) plain flour
½ cup (75g) self-raising flour
½ teaspoon bicarbonate of soda
½ teaspoon ground cinnamon
½ teaspoon ground ginger
1 cup (220g) firmly packed brown sugar
½ cup (40g) desiccated coconut
1 cup mashed banana
2 eggs, beaten lightly
¾ cup (180ml) vegetable oil
coconut crust
3 cups (225g) shredded coconut
½ cup (110g) firmly packed brown sugar
3 eggs, beaten lightly

**1** Preheat oven to 180°C/160°C fan-forced. Line 18 holes of two 12-hole standard muffin pans with paper cases.
**2** Drain pineapple over medium bowl, pressing with spoon to extract as much syrup as possible. Reserve ¼ cup of the syrup.
**3** Sift flours, soda, spices and sugar into large bowl. Stir in drained pineapple, reserved syrup, coconut, banana, egg and oil. Divide mixture into paper cases.
**4** Bake cakes 10 minutes.
**5** Meanwhile, make coconut crust.
**6** Spoon coconut crust over cakes; return to oven, bake about 15 minutes. Stand in pan 5 minutes; turn, top-side up, onto wire rack to cool. Serve dusted with sifted icing sugar.
**coconut crust** Combine ingredients in medium bowl.

tip You need two large overripe bananas (460g) for this amount of mashed bananas.

hummingbird cakes with coconut crust

caramel mud cakes

## TURKISH DELIGHTS

prep + cook time **1 hour (+ cooling)** makes **12**

60g white eating chocolate,
   chopped roughly
2 tablespoons rosewater
½ cup (125ml) water
⅓ cup (45g) pistachios
90g butter, softened
1 cup (220g) firmly packed brown sugar
2 eggs
⅔ cup (100g) self-raising flour
2 tablespoons plain flour
⅔ cup (90g) coarsely chopped
   pistachios, extra
300g white eating chocolate,
   melted, extra
900g turkish delight, chopped

**1** Preheat oven to 180°C/160°C fan-forced. Line 12-hole standard muffin pan with paper cases.
**2** Stir chocolate, rosewater and the water in small saucepan over low heat until smooth.
**3** Blend or process pistachios until fine.
**4** Beat butter, sugar and eggs in small bowl with electric mixer until combined.
**5** Fold in sifted flours, ground pistachios and warm chocolate mixture. Divide into cases.
**6** Bake cakes about 25 minutes. Turn cakes onto wire rack to cool.
**7** Cut a 3cm deep hole in the centre of each cake; fill with a few chopped extra nuts. Drizzle with a little extra melted chocolate; replace lids.
**8** Decorate cakes with pieces of turkish delight and chopped nuts dipped in melted chocolate.

**turkish delights**

## CARAMEL MUD CAKES

prep + cook time **45 minutes (+ cooling)** makes **12**

125g butter, chopped coarsely
100g white eating chocolate,
   chopped coarsely
⅔ cup (150g) firmly packed brown sugar
¼ cup (90g) golden syrup
⅔ cup (160ml) milk
1 cup (150g) plain flour
⅓ cup (50g) self-raising flour
1 egg
½ cup (80g) icing sugar

**1** Preheat oven to 160°C/140°C fan-forced. Line 12-hole standard muffin pan with paper cases.
**2** Stir butter, chocolate, sugar, syrup and milk in small saucepan over low heat until smooth. Transfer to medium bowl; cool 15 minutes.
**3** Whisk sifted flours then egg into chocolate mixture. Divide mixture into cases.
**4** Bake cakes about 30 minutes. Turn cakes, top-side up, onto wire rack to cool.
**5** Place doily, lace or stencil over cake; sift a little icing sugar over doily, then carefully lift doily from cake. Repeat with remaining cakes and icing sugar.

carrot cake kisses

## CARROT CAKE KISSES

prep + cook time **45 minutes**   makes **18**

1 cup (250ml) vegetable oil
1⅓ cups (300g) firmly packed brown sugar
3 eggs
3 cups firmly packed, coarsely grated carrot
1 cup (110g) coarsely chopped walnuts
2½ cups (375g) self-raising flour
½ teaspoon bicarbonate of soda
2 teaspoons mixed spice
90 milk chocolate kisses or milk Choc Bits
chocolate star sprinkles
cream cheese frosting
30g butter, softened
80g cream cheese, softened
1 ½ cups (240g) icing sugar

**1** Preheat oven to 180°C/160°C fan-forced.
Line 18 holes of two 12-hole standard muffin
pans with paper cases.
**2** Beat oil, sugar and eggs in small bowl with
electric mixer until thick. Transfer mixture to large
bowl; stir in carrot and nuts, then sifted dry
ingredients. Drop ¼ cup of mixture into cases.
**3** Bake about 30 minutes. Stand 5 minutes;
turn, top-side up, onto wire rack to cool.

**4** Meanwhile, make cream cheese frosting.
**5** Spread tops of cakes with frosting, decorate
with chocolate kisses and stars.
**cream cheese frosting**  Beat butter and cheese
in small bowl with electric mixer until light and
fluffy; gradually beat in sifted icing sugar.

## BUTTERFLY CAKES

prep + cook time **40 minutes**   makes **8**

1 cup (150g) self-raising flour
90g softened butter
1 teaspoon vanilla extract
½ cup (110g) caster sugar
2 eggs
2 tablespoons milk
1 tablespoon berry jam
¾ cup (180ml) thickened cream, whipped
1 teaspoon icing sugar

**1** Preheat oven to 180°C/160°C fan-forced.
Line eight holes of 12-hole standard muffin pan
with paper cases.
**2** Place sifted flour into small bowl with butter,
extract, sugar, eggs and milk; beat with electric
mixer on low speed until combined. Increase
speed to medium; beat until mixture changes to
a paler colour. Drop ¼ cup of mixture into cases.
**3** Bake about 20 minutes. Stand 5 minutes;
turn, top-side up, on wire rack to cool.
**4** Cut a round hole about 3cm deep in the
top of each cake. Halve the rounds of cake to
make butterfly wings.
**5** Fill each hole with jam, top with cream.
Position the wings on the cake, dust with
sifted icing sugar.

mini choc hazelnut cakes

# MINI CHOC HAZELNUT CAKES

prep + cook time **40 minutes (+ standing)** makes **12**

100g dark eating chocolate, chopped coarsely
¾ cup (180ml) water
100g butter, softened
1 cup (220g) firmly packed brown sugar
3 eggs
¼ cup (25g) cocoa powder
¾ cup (110g) self-raising flour
⅓ cup (35g) hazelnut meal
whipped hazelnut ganache
180g milk eating chocolate, chopped finely
⅓ cup (80ml) thickened cream
2 tablespoons hazelnut-flavoured liqueur

**1** Preheat oven to 180°C/160°C fan-forced.
Grease 12 x ½-cup (125ml) oval friand pans.
**2** Make whipped hazelnut ganache.
**3** Meanwhile, stir chocolate and the water in
medium saucepan over low heat until smooth.
**4** Beat butter and sugar in small bowl with
electric mixer until light and fluffy. Beat in eggs,
one at a time, until just combined (mixture may
separate at this stage, but will come together
later); transfer mixture to medium bowl. Stir in
warm chocolate mixture, sifted cocoa and flour,
and hazelnut meal. Divide mixture among pans.
**5** Bake about 20 minutes. Stand 5 minutes;
turn, top-sides up, onto wire rack to cool.
Spread ganache over cakes.
**whipped hazelnut ganache** Stir chocolate and
cream in small saucepan over low heat until
smooth. Stir in liqueur; transfer to small bowl.
Cover; stand 2 hours or until just firm. Beat
with electric mixer until pale brown in colour.

# CHOCOLATE RAINBOW CAKES

prep + cook time **50 minutes (+ cooling &
refrigeration)** makes **12**

60g dark eating chocolate, chopped coarsely
⅔ cup (160ml) water
90g softened butter
1 cup (220g) firmly packed brown sugar
2 eggs
⅔ cup (100g) self-raising flour
2 tablespoons cocoa powder

chocolate rainbow cakes

⅓ cup (40g) almond meal
½ cup smarties
¼ cup rainbow chips
chocolate ganache
½ cup (125ml) cream
200g dark eating chocolate, chopped coarsely

**1** Preheat oven to 170°C/150°C fan-forced. Line
12-hole muffin standard pan with paper cases.
**2** Make chocolate ganache.
**3** Meanwhile, stir chocolate and the water in
small saucepan over low heat until smooth.
**4** Beat butter, sugar and eggs in small bowl
with electric mixer until light and fluffy. Stir in
sifted flour and cocoa, meal and warm chocolate
mixture. Drop ¼ cup of mixture into cases.
**5** Bake about 25 minutes. Stand 5 minutes;
turn, top-side up, onto wire rack to cool.
**6** Fit a large piping bag with a large fluted tube,
half-fill the bag with ganache. Pipe swirls on each
cake, top with smarties and rainbow chips.
**chocolate ganache** Bring cream to the boil
in small saucepan; remove from heat. When
bubbles subside; stir in chocolate until smooth.
Transfer to small bowl; refrigerate 1 hour,
stirring occasionally, or until firm. Beat with
electric mixer until smooth.

choc top cupcakes

## LAMINGTON ANGEL CAKES

prep + cook time **45 minutes**  makes **12**

90g butter, softened
½ teaspoon vanilla extract
½ cup (110g) caster sugar
2 eggs
1 cup (150g) self-raising flour
2 tablespoons milk
1 cup (80g) desiccated coconut
¼ cup (80g) raspberry jam
½ cup (125ml) thickened cream, whipped
chocolate icing
10g butter
⅓ cup (80ml) milk
2 cups (320g) icing sugar
¼ cup (25g) cocoa powder

**1** Preheat oven to 180°C/160°C fan-forced.
Line 12-hole standard muffin pan with
paper cases.
**2** Combine butter, extract, sugar, eggs, flour
and milk in small bowl of electric mixer; beat on
low speed until ingredients are just combined.
Increase speed to medium; beat until mixture
is changed to a paler colour. Divide mixture into
cases; smooth surface.

**3** Bake cakes about 20 minutes. Turn cakes,
top-side up, onto wire rack to cool.
**4** Make chocolate icing.
**5** Remove cases from cakes. Dip cakes in
chocolate icing; drain off excess, toss cakes
in coconut. Place cakes on wire rack to set.
**6** Cut cakes as desired; fill with jam and cream.
**chocolate icing** Melt butter in medium
heatproof bowl over medium saucepan of
simmering water. Stir in milk and sifted icing
sugar and cocoa until icing is of a coating
consistency.

## CHOC TOP CUPCAKES

prep + cook time **45 minutes (+ standing)**  makes **24**

125g butter, softened
1 teaspoon vanilla extract
⅔ cup (150g) caster sugar
3 eggs
1½ cups (225g) self-raising flour
¼ cup (60ml) milk
100g dark eating chocolate, melted
100g white eating chocolate, melted
dark chocolate ganache
125g dark eating chocolate,
    chopped coarsely
⅓ cup (80ml) thickened cream

**1** Preheat oven to 180°C/160°C fan-forced. Line
two deep 12-hole patty pans with paper cases.
**2** Combine butter, extract, sugar, eggs, flour
and milk in small bowl of electric mixer; beat on
low speed until ingredients are just combined.
Increase speed to medium; beat 3 minutes or
until mixture is smooth and changed to a paler
colour. Divide mixture into cases
**3** Bake about 20 minutes. Turn cakes, top-side
up, onto wire rack to cool.
**4** Meanwhile, make dark chocolate ganache.
**5** Spread melted chocolates separately onto
a cold surface; when set, drag a melon baller
over the chocolate to make curls.
**6** Spread top of cakes with ganache. Arrange
chocolate curls on top of cakes.
**dark chocolate ganache** Stir ingredients in
small saucepan over low heat until smooth.
Cool to spreading consistency.

lamington angel cakes

apple custard tea cakes

## MOCHACCINOS

prep + cook time **1 hour 10 minutes (+ cooling)**
makes **12**

165g butter, chopped coarsely
100g dark eating chocolate,
  chopped coarsely
1⅓ cups (290g) caster sugar
⅔ cup (170ml) water
¼ cup (60ml) coffee liqueur
2 tablespoons instant coffee granules
1 cup (150g) plain flour
2 tablespoons self-raising flour
2 tablespoons cocoa powder
1 egg
300ml carton thickened cream, whipped
1 tablespoon cocoa powder, extra

**1** Preheat oven to 160°C/140°C fan-forced. Line 12-hole standard muffin pan with paper cases.
**2** Stir butter, chocolate, sugar, the water, liqueur and coffee in small saucepan over low heat until smooth. Transfer mixture to medium bowl; cool 15 minutes.
**3** Whisk sifted flours and cocoa into chocolate mixture, then egg. Divide mixture into cases.
**4** Bake cakes about 50 minutes. Turn cakes onto wire rack to cool.
**5** Remove cases from cakes. Place cakes in 125ml coffee cups, top with cream; dust with extra sifted cocoa.

mochaccinos

## APPLE CUSTARD TEA CAKES

prep + cook time **50 minutes (+ cooling)** makes **12**

90g butter
½ teaspoon vanilla extract
½ cup (110g) caster sugar
2 eggs
¾ cup (110g) self-raising flour
¼ cup (30g) custard powder
2 tablespoons milk
1 large unpeeled apple (200g), cored,
  sliced thinly
30g butter, melted
1 tablespoon caster sugar, extra
½ teaspoon ground cinnamon

**custard**
1 tablespoon custard powder
1 tablespoon caster sugar
½ cup (125ml) milk
¼ teaspoon vanilla extract

**1** Make custard.
**2** Preheat oven to 180°C/160°C fan-forced. Line 12-hole standard muffin pan with paper cases.
**3** Beat butter, extract, sugar, eggs, flour, custard powder and milk in small bowl of electric mixer on low speed until just combined. Increase speed to medium; beat until mixture is changed to a paler colour.
**4** Divide half the mixture into cases. Top with custard, then remaining cake mixture; spread mixture to cover custard. Top with apple slices, pressing slightly into cake.
**5** Bake cakes about 30 minutes.
**6** Brush hot cakes with extra butter; sprinkle with combined extra sugar and cinnamon. Turn cakes, top-side up, onto wire rack to cool.
**custard** Blend custard powder and sugar with milk and extract in small saucepan; stir over heat until mixture boils and thickens. Remove from heat; cover surface with plastic wrap; cool.

baby blue cupcakes

## BABY BLUE CUPCAKES

prep + cook time **50 minutes** makes **12**

60g dark eating chocolate,
    chopped coarsely
1 teaspoon finely grated orange rind
⅔ cup (160ml) orange juice
90g butter, softened
1 cup (220g) firmly packed brown sugar
2 eggs
⅔ cup (100g) self-raising flour
2 tablespoons cocoa powder
⅓ cup (40g) almond meal
½ cup (80g) icing sugar
400g ready-made white icing
blue food colouring
⅓ cup (110g) orange marmalade, warmed

1  Preheat oven to 160°C/150°C fan-forced. Line 12-hole standard muffin pan with paper cases.
2  Stir chocolate, rind and juice in small saucepan over low heat until smooth.
3  Beat butter, sugar and eggs in small bowl with electric mixer until light and fluffy. Stir in sifted flour and cocoa, almond meal and warm chocolate mixture. Divide mixture into cases; smooth surface.

4  Bake cakes about 25 minutes. Turn cakes onto wire rack to cool.
5  Dust surface with sifted icing sugar, knead ready-made icing until smooth. Knead blue colouring into icing.
6  Brush tops of cakes with strained marmalade. Roll icing out to 5mm thickness; cut rounds large enough to cover tops of cakes. Place rounds on cakes; tie cakes with ribbon.

## PATTY CAKES WITH GLACE ICING

prep + cook time **40 minutes** makes **12**

125g butter, softened
½ teaspoon vanilla extract
¾ cup (165g) caster sugar
3 eggs
2 cups (300g) self-raising flour
¼ cup (60ml) milk
glacé icing
2 cups (320g) icing sugar
20g butter, melted
2 tablespoons hot water, approximately

1  Preheat oven to 180°C/160°C fan-forced. Line 12-hole standard muffin pan with paper cases.
2  Place ingredients in medium bowl; beat with electric mixer on low speed until ingredients are combined. Increase speed to medium; beat about 3 minutes or until mixture is smooth and paler in colour. Divide mixture into paper cases.
3  Bake about 25 minutes. Stand 5 minutes; turn, top-side up, onto wire racks to cool.
4  Meanwhile, make glacé icing.
5  Spread cool cakes with icing.
**glacé icing** Sift icing sugar into small bowl; stir in butter and enough of the water to make a firm paste. Stir over small saucepan of simmering water until icing is spreadable.

**icing variations**
**coconut & lime** Stir in ½ teaspoon coconut essence and 1 teaspoon finely grated lime rind.
**orange** Stir in 1 teaspoon finely grated orange rind. Replace 1 tablespoon of the hot water with orange juice.
**passionfruit** Stir in 1 tablespoon passionfruit pulp.

patty cakes with glacé icing

carrot cupcakes with maple cream cheese frosting

## CARROT CUPCAKES WITH MAPLE CREAM CHEESE FROSTING

prep + cook time **45 minutes (+ cooling)** makes **12**

½ cup (125ml) vegetable oil
3 eggs
1½ cups (225g) self-raising flour
1 cup (220g) firmly packed brown sugar
2 teaspoons mixed spice
2 cups (480g) firmly packed coarsely
    grated carrot
¾ cup (90g) coarsely chopped roasted pecans
6 roasted pecans, halved
maple cream cheese frosting
30g butter, softened
80g cream cheese, softened
2 tablespoons maple syrup
1¼ cups (200g) icing sugar

**1** Preheat oven to 180°C/160°C fan-forced. Line 12-hole standard muffin pan with paper cases.
**2** Stir oil, eggs, sifted flour, sugar and spice in medium bowl until combined. Stir in carrot and chopped nuts. Divide mixture into paper cases.
**3** Bake about 30 minutes. Stand 5 minutes; turn, top-side up, onto wire rack to cool.
**4** Meanwhile, make maple cream cheese frosting.
**5** Spread frosting over cakes; top with a nut.
**maple cream cheese frosting** Beat butter, cream cheese and syrup in small bowl with electric mixer until light and fluffy; gradually beat in sifted icing sugar until spreadable.

tip **You need four medium carrots (480g) for the required amount of grated carrot.**

## DAISY CAKES

prep + cook time **45 minutes** makes **24**

125g butter, softened
1 teaspoon vanilla extract
⅔ cup (150g) caster sugar
3 eggs
1½ cups (225g) self-raising flour
¼ cup (60ml) milk
60 pink marshmallows
24 red smarties

daisy cakes

vanilla butter cream
125g butter, softened
1 teaspoon vanilla extract
1½ cups (240g) icing sugar
2 tablespoons milk

**1** Preheat oven to 180°C/160°C fan-forced. Line two deep 12-hole patty pans with paper cases.
**2** Beat butter, extract, sugar, egg, sifted flour and milk in small bowl of electric mixer on low speed until ingredients just combine. Increase speed to medium; beat about 3 minutes or until mixture is smooth and changed to a paler colour. Divide mixture into cases.
**3** Bake about 20 minutes. Turn cakes, top-side up, onto wire rack to cool.
**4** Meanwhile, make vanilla butter cream.
**5** Spread tops of cakes with butter cream. Cut marshmallows in half horizontally; squeeze ends together to form petals. Decorate cakes with petals; position a smartie in the centre of each daisy.
**vanilla butter cream** Beat butter and extract in small bowl with electric mixer until as white as possible. Gradually beat in half the sifted icing sugar, milk, then remaining icing sugar.

coconut cherry hearts

4 Make milk chocolate ganache.
5 Divide white chocolate among three small bowls; tint two portions in different shades of pink. Pipe different coloured heart shapes onto baking-paper-lined tray. Set at room temperature.
6 Spread cakes with ganache; top with hearts.
**milk chocolate ganache** Bring cream to the boil in small saucepan; pour over chocolate in small bowl, stir until smooth. Cover; stand at room temperature until spreadable.

## WHITE CHOCOLATE MUD CAKES

prep + cook time **1 hour 10 minutes**  makes **24**

250g butter, chopped coarsely
150g white eating chocolate, chopped
2 cups (440g) caster sugar
1 cup (250ml) milk
1½ cups (225g) plain flour
½ cup (75g) self-raising flour
1 teaspoon vanilla extract
2 eggs, beaten lightly
small flowers and silver cachous
fluffy frosting
1 cup (220g) caster sugar
⅓ cup (80ml) water
2 egg whites

1 Preheat oven to 160°C/140°C fan-forced. Line two 12-hole muffin pans with paper cases.
2 Stir butter, chocolate, sugar and milk in pan over low heat, without boiling, until smooth. Transfer to medium bowl; cool 15 minutes.
3 Whisk sifted flours, then extract and egg into chocolate mixture. Divide mixture into cases.
4 Bake cakes about 35 minutes. Turn cakes, top-side up, onto wire rack to cool.
5 Make fluffy frosting. Spread cakes with frosting; decorate with flowers and cachous.
**fluffy frosting** Stir sugar and the water in small saucepan over heat, without boiling, until sugar is dissolved. Boil, uncovered, without stirring, 5 minutes or until syrup reaches 116°C on a candy thermometer. Syrup should be thick but not coloured. Remove from heat, allow bubbles to subside. Beat egg whites in small bowl with electric mixer until soft peaks form. While motor is operating, add hot syrup in a thin stream; beat on high speed 10 minutes or until thick.

## COCONUT CHERRY HEARTS

prep + cook time **50 minutes**  makes **12**

125g butter, softened
½ teaspoon coconut essence
⅔ cup (150g) caster sugar
2 eggs
⅓ cup (80ml) milk
½ cup (40g) desiccated coconut
⅓ cup (70g) red glacé cherries, chopped coarsely
50g dark eating chocolate, chopped
1 cup (150g) self-raising flour
¼ cup (35g) plain flour
150g white chocolate Melts, melted
pink food colouring
milk chocolate ganache
¼ cup (60ml) cream
100g milk eating chocolate, chopped

1 Preheat oven to 180°C/160°C fan-forced. Line 12-hole standard muffin pan with paper cases.
2 Beat butter, essence, sugar and eggs in small bowl with electric mixer until combined. Stir in milk, coconut, cherries and chocolate, then sifted flours. Divide among cases; smooth surface.
3 Bake cakes about 25 minutes. Turn, top-side up, onto wire rack to cool.

white chocolate mud cakes

very berry cakes

## CHANTILLY CREAM & BERRY CUPCAKES

prep + cook time **35 minutes**  makes **8**

1 cup (150g) self-raising flour
90g softened butter
1 teaspoon vanilla extract
½ cup (110g) caster sugar
2 eggs
2 tablespoons milk
1 cup (150g) mixed fresh berries
chantilly cream
¾ cup (180ml) thickened cream
1 tablespoon icing sugar
½ teaspoon of vanilla extract

**1** Preheat oven to 180°C/160°C fan-forced.
Line eight holes of 12-hole standard muffin pan
with paper cases.
**2** Sift flour into small bowl, add butter, extract,
sugar, eggs and milk; beat with electric mixer
on low speed until ingredients are just
combined. Increase speed to medium; beat
until mixture is changed to a paler colour.
Drop ¼ cup of mixture into paper cases.
**3** Bake cakes about 20 minutes. Stand in
pan 5 minutes; turn, top-side up, onto wire
rack to cool.
**4** Meanwhile, make chantilly cream
**5** Spread cakes with cream; top with berries.
Dust with a little sifted icing sugar
**chantilly cream** Beat ingredients in small bowl
with electric mixer until thick.

## VERY BERRY CAKES

prep + cook time **1 hour 10 minutes (+ standing)**
makes **12**

125g butter, softened
½ teaspoon vanilla extract
⅔ cup (150g) caster sugar
2 eggs
1 cup (150g) dried mixed berries
½ cup (70g) slivered almonds
⅔ cup (100g) plain flour
⅓ cup (50g) self-raising flour
¼ cup (60ml) milk

chantilly cream & berry cupcakes

sugared fruit
150g fresh blueberries
120g fresh raspberries
1 egg white, beaten lightly
2 tablespoons vanilla sugar
cream cheese frosting
30g butter, softened
80g cream cheese, softened
1½ cups (240g) icing sugar

**1** Prepare sugared fruit.
**2** Preheat oven to 160°C/140°C fan-forced. Line
12-hole standard muffin pan with paper cases.
**3** Beat butter, extract, sugar and eggs in small
bowl with electric mixer until light and fluffy.
Stir in fruit and nuts, then sifted flours and milk.
Divide mixture into cases; smooth surface.
**4** Bake cakes about 35 minutes. Turn cakes,
top-side up, onto wire rack to cool.
**5** Make cream cheese frosting. Spread cakes
with frosting; decorate with sugared fruit.
**sugared fruit** Brush each berry with egg white;
roll in vanilla sugar. Place fruit on baking-paper-
lined tray. Leave 1 hour or until sugar is dry.
**cream cheese frosting** Beat butter and cream
cheese in small bowl with electric mixer until light
and fluffy; gradually beat in sifted icing sugar.

passionfruit curd cakes

3 Bake about 20 minutes. Stand 5 minutes; turn, top-side up, onto wire rack to cool.
4 Meanwhile, make butter cream.
5 Break flake bar into pieces; stir one third into butter cream. Spread cakes with butter cream, then melted chocolate. Top with remaining flake.
**butter cream** Beat butter in small bowl with electric mixer until as white as possible; beat in sifted icing sugar and milk, in two batches. Tint butter cream green, flavour with a little essence.

## PASSIONFRUIT CURD CAKES

prep + cook time **50 minutes (+ refrigeration & cooling)** makes **12**

90g butter, softened
½ cup (110g) caster sugar
2 eggs
1 cup (150g) self-raising flour
¼ cup (60ml) passionfruit pulp
85g packet passionfruit jelly
1 cup (250ml) boiling water
1 cup (80g) desiccated coconut
½ cup (125ml) thickened cream, whipped
passionfruit curd
2 eggs, beaten lightly
⅓ cup (75g) caster sugar
1 tablespoon lemon juice
¼ cup (60ml) passionfruit pulp
60g butter, chopped coarsely

1 Make passionfruit curd.
2 Preheat oven to 180°C/160°C fan-forced. Line 12-hole standard muffin pan with paper cases.
3 Beat butter, sugar, eggs and flour in small bowl of electric mixer on low speed until just combined. Increase speed to medium; beat until changed to a paler colour. Stir in pulp. Divide mixture into cases; smooth surface.
4 Bake about 20 minutes. Turn, top-side up, onto wire rack to cool.
5 Dissolve jelly in the boiling water. Refrigerate 30 minutes (should look like unbeaten egg white).
6 Remove cases from cakes. Roll cakes in jelly; stand in jelly 15 minutes, turning occasionally. Roll cakes in coconut; place on wire rack over tray. Refrigerate 30 minutes.
7 Cut cakes in half; fill with curd and cream.
**passionfruit curd** Stir ingredients in small heatproof bowl over small pan of simmering water, constantly, until slightly thickened. Remove from heat. Cover tightly; refrigerate until cold.

## CHOCOLATE PEPPERMINT CAKES

prep + cook time **45 minutes** makes **15**

1 cup (150g) self-raising flour
½ cup (75g) plain flour
⅓ cup (35g) cocoa powder
¾ cup (165g) caster sugar
185g softened butter
3 eggs
½ cup (125ml) milk
1 Flake bar
100g milk Choc Melts, melted
butter cream
125g butter, softened
1½ cups (240g) icing sugar
2 tablespoons milk
green food colouring
peppermint essence

1 Preheat oven to 180°C/160°C fan-forced. Line 15 holes of two 12-hole standard muffin pans with paper cases.
2 Sift dry ingredients into medium large bowl, add remaining ingredients; beat with electric mixer on low speed until ingredients are . combined. Increase speed to medium; beat until mixture is smooth and has changed to a paler colour. Drop ¼ cup of mixture into cases.

banana caramel cakes

## BANANA CARAMEL CAKES

prep + cook time **45 minutes** makes **12**

90g butter, softened
½ cup (110g) firmly packed brown sugar
2 eggs
½ cup (75g) self-raising flour
½ cup (75g) plain flour
½ teaspoon bicarbonate of soda
½ teaspoon mixed spice
⅔ cup mashed overripe banana
⅓ cup (80g) sour cream
2 tablespoons milk
380g can Top 'n' Fill caramel
½ cup (125ml) thickened cream, whipped
2 medium bananas (400g), extra, sliced thinly
100g dark eating chocolate

**1** Preheat oven to 180°C/160°C fan-forced. Line
12-hole standard muffin pan with paper cases.
**2** Beat butter, sugar and eggs in small bowl
with electric mixer until light and fluffy. Stir in
sifted dry ingredients, banana, sour cream and
milk. Divide mixture into cases; smooth surface.
**3** Bake cakes about 20 minutes. Turn cakes
onto wire rack to cool. Remove cases from cakes.
**4** Fold 2 tablespoons of the caramel into cream.
**5** Cut cakes horizontally into three slices. Re-
assemble cakes with remaining caramel and
banana. Top with caramel-flavoured cream.
**6** Using a vegetable peeler, grate chocolate;
sprinkle over cakes.

## CHOCOLATE & COCONUT SPONGE

prep + cook time **35 minutes** makes **18**

4 eggs
¾ cup (165g) caster sugar
⅔ cup (100g) self-raising flour
⅓ cup (35g) cocoa powder
90g butter, melted
1 tablespoon hot water
⅔ cup (160ml) thickened cream
2 tablespoons caster sugar, extra
⅓ cup (15g) flaked coconut
chocolate ganache
200g dark eating chocolate, chopped
⅔ cup (160ml) thickened cream

chocolate & coconut sponge

**1** Preheat oven to 180°C/160°C fan-forced.
Grease two 9-hole friand pans.
**2** Beat eggs in small bowl with electric mixer
about 8 minutes until thick and creamy. Beat in
sugar, a tablespoon at a time, until dissolved.
Transfer mixture to large bowl. Fold in sifted
flour and cocoa, then butter and the hot water.
Divide mixture among pan holes.
**3** Bake about 12 minutes or until sponges
spring back when touched lightly. Turn cakes,
top-side up, onto wire rack to cool.
**4** Meanwhile, make chocolate ganache.
**5** Beat cream and extra sugar in small bowl
with electric mixer until soft peaks form. Split
cooled sponges in half. Spread bases with
cream; replace tops.
**6** Spread chocolate ganache over cakes then
sprinkle with coconut.
**chocolate ganache** Stir ingredients in small
saucepan over low heat until smooth. Cool to
spreading consistency.

chocolate ginger cakes with honeycomb cream

## CHOCOLATE GINGER CAKES WITH HONEYCOMB CREAM

prep + cook time **45 minutes**  makes **12**

½ cup (110g) firmly packed brown sugar
½ cup (75g) plain flour
½ cup (75g) self-raising flour
¼ teaspoon bicarbonate of soda
1 teaspoon ground ginger
½ teaspoon ground cinnamon
¼ teaspoon ground nutmeg
90g butter, softened
1 egg
¼ cup (60ml) buttermilk
2 tablespoons golden syrup
50g dark eating chocolate,
    chopped coarsely
300ml thickened cream, whipped
3 x 50g Violet Crumble bars,
    chopped coarsely

**1** Preheat oven to 160°C/140°C fan-forced.
Line 12-hole standard muffin pan with
paper cases.
**2** Sift dry ingredients into small bowl of electric
mixer; add butter, egg, buttermilk and syrup,
beat on low speed until ingredients are
combined. Increase speed to medium; beat
until mixture is changed to a paler colour.
Stir in chocolate. Divide mixture into cases;
smooth surface.
**3** Bake cakes about 30 minutes. Turn cakes,
top-side up, onto wire rack to cool.
**4** Spread cakes with whipped cream; top with
chopped honeycomb.

## GLUTEN-FREE BERRY CUPCAKES

prep + cook time **40 minutes**  makes **12**

125g butter, softened
2 teaspoons finely grated lemon rind
¾ cup (165g) caster sugar
4 eggs
2 cups (240g) almond meal
½ cup (40g) desiccated coconut
½ cup (100g) rice flour
1 teaspoon bicarbonate of soda
1 cup (150g) frozen mixed berries
1 tablespoon desiccated coconut, extra

**1** Preheat oven to 180°C/160°C fan-forced. Line
12-hole standard muffin pan with paper cases.
**2** Beat butter, rind and sugar in small bowl with
electric mixer until light and fluffy. Beat in eggs,
one at a time, until just combined (mixture may
separate at this stage, but will come together
later); transfer to large bowl. Stir in almond
meal, coconut, sifted flour and soda, then
berries. Divide mixture into cases.
**3** Bake cakes about 25 minutes. Stand cakes
in pan 5 minutes; turn, top-side up, onto wire
rack to cool. Sprinkle with extra coconut.

gluten-free berry cupcakes

chocolate, date & almond meringues

## CHOCOLATE, DATE & ALMOND MERINGUES

prep + cook time 1 hour 10 minutes (+ cooling & standing) makes 20

6 egg whites
1½ cups (330g) caster sugar
2 teaspoons 100% corn cornflour
1 cup (150g) finely chopped dried dates
150g dark eating chocolate, chopped finely
1 cup (160g) almond kernels, roasted, chopped coarsely
125g dark eating chocolate, extra, melted
24 almond kernels, extra

1  Preheat oven to 140°C/120°C fan-forced. Line 20 holes of two 12-hole standard muffin pans with paper cases.
2  Beat egg whites in large bowl with electric mixer until soft peaks form; gradually add sugar, beat until dissolved between additions. Gently and quickly fold in cornflour, dates, chocolate and chopped almonds. Divide mixture into cases.
3  Bake meringues about 50 minutes or until dry to touch. Cool in oven with door ajar.
4  Spread tops with extra melted chocolate, top each meringue with an extra almond. Stand until set.

## BLACK FOREST CAKES

prep + cook time 1 hour 20 minutes (+ cooling) makes 12

425g can pitted cherries in syrup
165g butter, chopped coarsely
100g dark eating chocolate, chopped coarsely
1⅓ cups (295g) caster sugar
¼ cup (60ml) cherry brandy
1 cup (150g) plain flour
2 tablespoons self-raising flour
2 tablespoons cocoa powder
1 egg
⅔ cup (160ml) thickened cream, whipped
2 teaspoons cherry brandy, extra
100g dark eating chocolate, left whole

black forest cakes

1  Preheat oven to 160°C/140°C fan-forced. Line 12-hole standard muffin pan with paper cases.
2  Drain cherries; reserve syrup. Process ½ cup cherries with ½ cup syrup until smooth. Halve remaining cherries; reserve for decorating cakes. Discard remaining syrup.
3  Stir butter, chocolate, sugar, brandy and cherry puree in small saucepan over low heat until chocolate is melted. Transfer mixture to medium bowl; cool 15 minutes.
4  Whisk sifted flours and cocoa into chocolate mixture, then egg. Divide mixture into cases; smooth surface.
5  Bake cakes about 45 minutes. Turn cakes, top-side up, onto wire rack to cool.
6  Combine cream and extra cherry brandy in small bowl. Top cakes with remaining cherry halves then brandy cream. Using sharp vegetable peeler, scrape down the long side of chocolate to make small chocolate curls; sprinkle over cakes.

tip  The chocolate will curl much easier if it is at room temperature.

## CHRISTMAS PUDDING COOKIES

**prep + cook time** 55 minutes (+ refrigeration & standing) **makes** 30

1⅔ cups (250g) plain flour
⅓ cup (40g) almond meal
⅓ cup (75g) caster sugar
1 teaspoon mixed spice
1 teaspoon vanilla extract
125g cold butter, chopped
2 tablespoons water
700g rich dark fruit cake
⅓ cup (80ml) brandy
1 egg white
400g dark eating chocolate, melted
½ cup (75g) white chocolate Melts, melted
30 red glacé cherries

1 Process flour, meal, sugar, spice, extract and butter until crumbly. Add the water, process until ingredients come together.
2 Knead dough on floured surface until smooth; roll dough between sheets of baking paper until 5mm thick. Cover; refrigerate 30 minutes.
3 Preheat oven to 180°C/160°C fan-forced. Grease oven trays; line with baking paper.
4 Using 5.5cm round cutter, cut 30 rounds from dough. Place about 3cm apart on oven trays.
5 Bake cookies about 10 minutes.
6 Meanwhile, crumble fruit cake into a medium bowl; add brandy. Press mixture firmly into round metal tablespoon measures. Brush partially baked cookies with egg white, top with cake domes; bake further 5 minutes. Cool on wire racks.
7 Place wire racks over oven tray, coat cookies with dark chocolate; set at room temperature.
8 Spoon white chocolate over cookies; top with cherries.

COOKIES

melt-in-the-mouth vanilla biscuits

## MELT-IN-THE-MOUTH VANILLA BISCUITS

prep + cook time **30 minutes (+ refrigeration)**
makes **60**

180g butter, softened
1 teaspoon vanilla bean paste
1 cup (160g) icing sugar
1½ tablespoons milk
1¾ cups (260g) plain flour
2 tablespoons cornflour

**1** Preheat oven to 160°C/140°C fan-forced. Grease oven trays.
**2** Beat butter, vanilla and ⅓ cup sifted icing sugar in small bowl with electric mixer until light and fluffy. Add milk; beat until combined.
**3** Add sifted flour and cornflour; beat on low speed until combined.
**4** Refrigerate biscuit dough about 10 minutes or until firm enough to roll.
**5** Roll dough into a 30cm log; wrap in plastic. Refrigerate dough 1 hour.
**6** Cut dough into 4mm slices. Place slices on trays 3cm apart.
**7** Bake biscuits about 10 minutes or until just golden. Stand biscuits on trays 5 minutes; transfer to wire racks to cool slightly. While still warm, dust biscuits liberally with remaining sifted icing sugar. Cool completely on wire racks.

tip **If vanilla bean paste is hard to find, you can use 3 teaspoons vanilla extract instead.**

## COCONUT FORTUNE COOKIES

prep + cook time **35 minutes (+ cooling)** makes **12**

2 egg whites
⅓ cup (75g) caster sugar
⅓ cup (50g) plain flour
1 teaspoon coconut essence
30g butter, melted
½ teaspoon finely grated lime rind
2 tablespoons desiccated coconut

**1** Preheat oven to 160°C/140°C fan-forced. Grease oven tray; line with baking paper. Mark two 9cm circles on paper.
**2** Beat egg whites in small bowl with electric mixer until soft peaks form; gradually beat in sugar, beating until dissolved between additions. Fold in sifted flour, essence, butter and rind.
**3** Drop one level tablespoon of mixture into centre of each circle on oven tray, spread evenly to cover circle completely; sprinkle with a little coconut. Bake about 5 minutes.
**4** Working quickly, loosen cookies from tray, place small paper message in the centre of cookies; fold in half then gently bend cookies over edge of a glass. Cool 30 seconds. Place on wire rack to cool. Repeat with remaining mixture and coconut.

coconut fortune cookies

gingernuts

# PISTACHIO SHORTBREAD MOUNDS

prep + cook time **40 minutes** makes **40**

**½ cup (75g) shelled pistachios, roasted**
**250g butter, chopped**
**1 cup (160g) icing sugar**
**1½ cups (225g) plain flour**
**2 tablespoons rice flour**
**2 tablespoons cornflour**
**¾ cup (90g) almond meal**
**⅓ cup (55g) icing sugar, extra**

**1** Preheat oven to 150°C/130°C fan-forced. Grease oven trays.
**2** Coarsely chop ⅓ cup of the nuts; leave remaining nuts whole.
**3** Beat butter and icing sugar in small bowl with electric mixer until light and fluffy; transfer mixture to large bowl. Stir in sifted flours, almond meal and chopped nuts.
**4** Shape level tablespoons of mixture into mounds; place mounds on trays, allowing 3cm between each mound. Press one reserved nut onto each mound.
**5** Bake about 25 minutes or until firm; stand mounds 5 minutes before transferring to wire rack to cool.
**6** Serve mounds dusted with extra sifted icing sugar.

pistachio shortbread mounds

# GINGERNUTS

prep + cook time **20 minutes (+ cooling)** makes **32**

**90g butter**
**⅓ cup (75g) firmly packed brown sugar**
**⅓ cup (115g) golden syrup**
**1⅓ cups (200g) plain flour**
**¾ teaspoon bicarbonate of soda**
**1 tablespoon ground ginger**
**1 teaspoon ground cinnamon**
**¼ teaspoon ground clove**

**1** Preheat oven to 180°C/160°C fan-forced. Grease oven trays.
**2** Stir butter, sugar and syrup in medium saucepan over low heat until smooth. Remove pan from heat; stir in sifted dry ingredients. Cool 10 minutes.
**3** Roll rounded teaspoons of mixture into balls. Place about 3cm apart on trays; flatten slightly.
**4** Bake about 10 minutes; cool on trays.

oat & bran biscuits

## DOUBLE CHOCOLATE FRECKLES

prep + cook time **40 minutes (+ refrigeration & standing)** makes **42**

125g butter, softened
¾ cup (165g) firmly packed brown sugar
1 egg
1½ cups (225g) plain flour
¼ cup (35g) self-raising flour
¼ cup (35g) cocoa powder
200g dark eating chocolate, melted
⅓ cup (85g) hundreds and thousands

**1** Beat butter, sugar and egg in small bowl with electric mixer until combined. Stir in sifted dry ingredients, in two batches.
**2** Knead dough on floured surface until smooth; roll between sheets of baking paper until 5mm thick. Cover; refrigerate 30 minutes.
**3** Preheat oven to 180°C/160°C fan-forced. Grease oven trays; line with baking paper.
**4** Using 3cm, 5cm and 6.5cm round cutters, cut 14 rounds from dough using each cutter. Place 3cm rounds on one oven tray; place remainder on other oven trays.
**5** Bake small cookies about 10 minutes; bake larger cookies about 12 minutes. Cool on wire racks.
**6** Spread tops of cookies with chocolate; sprinkle with hundreds and thousands. Set at room temperature.

## OAT & BRAN BISCUITS

prep + cook time **35 minutes (+ refrigeration)** makes **30**

1 cup (150g) plain flour
1 cup (70g) unprocessed bran
¾ cup (65g) rolled oats
½ teaspoon bicarbonate of soda
60g butter, chopped
½ cup (110g) caster sugar
1 egg
2 tablespoons water, approximately

**1** Process flour, bran, oats, soda and butter until crumbly; add sugar, egg and enough of the water to make a firm dough.
**2** Knead dough on lightly floured surface until smooth; cover, refrigerate 30 minutes.
**3** Preheat oven to 180°C/160°C fan-forced. Grease oven trays; line with baking paper.
**4** Divide dough in half; roll each half between sheets of baking paper to about 5mm thickness. Cut dough into 7cm rounds; place on trays 2cm apart.
**5** Bake biscuits about 15 minutes. Stand on trays 5 minutes; transfer to wire rack to cool.

double chocolate freckles

anzacs

## ANZACS

prep + cook time **35 minutes**  makes **25**

1 cup (90g) rolled oats
1 cup (150g) plain flour
1 cup (220g) firmly packed brown sugar
½ cup (40g) desiccated coconut
125g butter
2 tablespoons golden syrup
1 tablespoon water
½ teaspoon bicarbonate of soda

**1**  Preheat oven to 160°C/140°C fan-forced.
Grease oven trays; line with baking paper.
**2**  Combine oats, sifted flour, sugar and
coconut in large bowl.
**3**  Stir butter, syrup and the water in small
saucepan over low heat until smooth; stir in
soda. Stir syrup mixture into dry ingredients.
**4**  Roll level tablespoons of mixture into balls;
place about 5cm apart on trays, flatten slightly.
**5**  Bake about 20 minutes; cool on trays.

mini florentines

## MINI FLORENTINES

prep + cook time **20 minutes (+ standing)**  makes **25**

¾ cup (120g) sultanas
2 cups (80g) cornflakes
¾ cup (60g) roasted flaked almonds
½ cup (100g) red glacé cherries
⅔ cup (160ml) sweetened condensed milk
60g white eating chocolate, melted
60g dark eating chocolate, melted

**1**  Preheat oven to 180°C/160°C fan-forced.
Grease oven trays; line with baking paper.
**2**  Combine sultanas, cornflakes, nuts, cherries
and condensed milk in medium bowl.
**3**  Drop level tablespoons of mixture about
5cm apart on trays.
**4**  Bake florentines 5 minutes; cool on trays.
**5**  Spread bases of half the florentines with
white chocolate; spread remaining half with
dark chocolate. Run fork through chocolate to
make waves; allow to set at room temperature.

**almond macaroons**

## JAMMY FLOWERS

prep + cook time **35 minutes** makes **26**

125g butter, softened
½ teaspoon vanilla extract
½ cup (110g) caster sugar
1 cup (120g) almond meal
1 egg
1 cup (150g) plain flour
1 teaspoon finely grated lemon rind
⅓ cup (110g) raspberry jam
2 tablespoons apricot jam

**1** Preheat oven to 180°C/160°C fan-forced. Grease oven trays; line with baking paper.
**2** Beat butter, extract, sugar and almond meal in small bowl with electric mixer until light and fluffy. Add egg, beat until combined; stir in sifted flour.
**3** Divide rind between both jams; mix well.
**4** Roll level tablespoons of mixture into balls; place about 5cm apart on oven trays, flatten slightly. Using end of a wooden spoon, press a flower shape (about 1cm deep) into dough; fill each hole with a little jam, using apricot jam for centres of flowers.
**5** Bake about 15 minutes. Cool on trays.

## ALMOND MACAROONS

prep + cook time **35 minutes** makes **22**

2 egg whites
½ cup (110g) caster sugar
1¼ cups (150g) almond meal
½ teaspoon almond essence
2 tablespoons plain flour
¼ cup (40g) blanched almond

**1** Preheat oven to 150°C/130°C fan-forced. Grease oven trays.
**2** Beat egg whites in small bowl with electric mixer until soft peaks form; gradually add sugar, beating until dissolved between additions. Gently fold in meal, essence and sifted flour, in two batches.
**3** Drop level tablespoons of mixture about 5cm apart on trays; press one nut onto each macaroon.
**4** Bake macaroons about 20 minutes or until firm and dry; cool on trays.

### variations
**coconut** Replace almond meal with ¾ cup desiccated coconut and ¾ cup shredded coconut. Replace almond essence with vanilla extract; omit blanched almonds.
**strawberry coconut** Replace almond meal with 1½ cups shredded coconut. Replace almond essence with vanilla extract; omit blanched almonds. Fold ⅓ cup finely chopped dried strawberries into the basic mixture.

jammy flowers

orange hazelnut butter yoyo bites

## ORANGE HAZELNUT BUTTER YOYO BITES

prep + cook time 30 minutes (+ cooling) makes 20

250g unsalted butter, softened
1 teaspoon vanilla extract
½ cup (80g) icing sugar
1½ cups (225g) plain flour
½ cup (75g) cornflour
orange hazelnut butter
80g unsalted butter, softened
2 teaspoons finely grated orange rind
⅔ cup (110g) icing sugar
1 tablespoon hazelnut meal

vanilla kisses

**1** Preheat oven to 160°C/140°C fan-forced. Grease oven trays; line with baking paper.
**2** Beat butter, extract and sifted icing sugar in small bowl with electric mixer until light and fluffy; stir in sifted dry ingredients, in two batches.
**3** Roll rounded teaspoons of mixture into balls; place about 3cm apart on trays. Using fork dusted with flour, press tines gently onto each biscuit to flatten slightly.
**4** Bake about 15 minutes; cool on trays.
**5** Meanwhile, make orange hazelnut butter.
**6** Sandwich biscuits with orange hazelnut butter; dust with extra sifted icing sugar.
**orange hazelnut butter** Beat butter, rind and sifted icing sugar in small bowl with electric mixer until light and fluffy. Stir in meal.

## VANILLA KISSES

prep + cook time 25 minutes (+ cooling) makes 20

125g butter, softened
½ cup (110g) caster sugar
1 egg
⅓ cup (50g) plain flour
¼ cup (35g) self-raising flour
⅔ cup (100g) cornflour
¼ cup (30g) custard powder
vienna cream
60g butter, softened
½ teaspoon vanilla extract
¾ cup (120g) icing sugar
2 teaspoons milk

**1** Preheat oven to 200°C/180°C fan-forced. Grease oven trays; line with baking paper.
**2** Beat butter, sugar and egg in small bowl with electric mixer until light and fluffy. Stir in sifted dry ingredients, in two batches.
**3** Spoon mixture into piping bag fitted with 1cm-fluted tube. Pipe 3cm rosettes about 3cm apart on trays.
**4** Bake about 10 minutes; cool on trays.
**5** Meanwhile, make vienna cream.
**6** Sandwich biscuits with vienna cream.
**vienna cream** Beat butter and extract in small bowl with electric mixer until as white as possible; gradually beat in sifted icing sugar and milk, in two batches.

**hot cross bun cookies**

## HOT CROSS BUN COOKIES

prep + cook time **40 minutes** makes **48**

125g butter, softened
⅔ cup (150g) caster sugar
1 egg
¼ cup (40g) finely chopped mixed peel
½ cup (80g) dried currants
2 cups (300g) self-raising flour
1 teaspoon mixed spice
2 teaspoons milk
2 tablespoons almond meal
100g marzipan
2 tablespoons apricot jam, warmed, strained

**1** Preheat oven to 160°C/140°C fan-forced. Grease oven trays; line with baking paper.
**2** Beat butter, sugar and egg in small bowl with electric mixer until light and fluffy. Stir in peel, currants, sifted flour and spice, and milk in two batches.
**3** Roll rounded teaspoons of mixture into balls; place about 5cm apart on oven trays.
**4** Knead almond meal into marzipan. Roll marzipan into 5mm diameter sausages; cut into 4cm lengths.
**5** Brush cookies with a little milk; place marzipan lengths on cookies to make crosses, press down gently.
**6** Bake cookies about 15 minutes. Brush cookies with jam; cool on trays.

## SHORTBREAD BUTTONS

prep + cook time **45 minutes** makes **26**

250g butter, softened
⅓ cup (75g) caster sugar
¼ cup (35g) rice flour
2¼ cups (335g) plain flour
1 tablespoon caster sugar, extra

**1** Preheat oven to 150°C/130°C fan-forced. Grease oven trays; line with baking paper.
**2** Beat butter and sugar in small bowl with electric mixer until smooth. Stir in sifted flours. Knead dough on floured surface until smooth.
**3** Place 5cm round floured cutter on an oven tray, press one level tablespoon of dough evenly inside the cutter, remove cutter. Repeat with remaining dough.
**4** Use the lid of a plastic water bottle to indent the buttons. Use a skewer to make holes in buttons. Use a fork to make pattern around edges of buttons. Sprinkle with extra sugar.
**5** Bake 30 minutes or until firm. Cool on trays.

shortbread buttons

hazelnut pinwheels

## HAZELNUT PINWHEELS

prep + cook time **40 minutes (+ refrigeration)**
makes **30**

**1¼ cups (175g) plain flour**
**100g butter, chopped**
**½ cup (110g) caster sugar**
**1 egg yolk**
**1 tablespoon milk, approximately**
**⅓ cup (110g) chocolate hazelnut spread**
**2 tablespoons hazelnut meal**

**1** Process flour, butter and sugar until crumbly.
Add egg yolk; process with enough milk until
mixture forms a ball. Knead dough on floured
surface until smooth. Cover; refrigerate 1 hour.
**2** Preheat oven to 180°C/160°C fan-forced.
Grease oven trays; line with baking paper.
**3** Roll dough between sheets of baking paper
to form 20cm x 30cm rectangle; remove top
sheet of paper. Spread dough evenly with
hazelnut spread; sprinkle with hazelnut meal.
Using paper as a guide, roll dough tightly from
long side to enclose filling. Enclose roll in
plastic wrap; refrigerate 30 minutes.
**4** Remove plastic; cut roll into 1cm slices,
place slices on trays 2cm apart.
**5** Bake pinwheels about 20 minutes. Stand on
trays 5 minutes; transfer to wire rack to cool.

triple-choc cookies

## TRIPLE-CHOC COOKIES

prep + cook time **30 minutes** makes **36**

**125g butter, chopped**
**½ teaspoon vanilla extract**
**1¼ cups (275g) firmly packed brown sugar**
**1 egg**
**1 cup (150g) plain flour**
**¼ cup (35g) self-raising flour**
**1 teaspoon bicarbonate of soda**
**⅓ cup (35g) cocoa powder**
**½ cup (85g) coarsely chopped raisins**
**½ cup (95g) milk Choc Bits**
**½ cup (75g) white chocolate Melts, halved**
**½ cup (75g) dark chocolate Melts, halved**

**1** Preheat oven to 180°C/160°C fan-forced.
Grease oven trays.
**2** Beat butter, extract, sugar and egg in small
bowl with electric mixer until smooth; do not
overbeat. Stir in sifted dry ingredients, then
raisins and all the chocolate. Drop level
tablespoons of mixture 5cm apart onto trays.
**3** Bake cookies about 10 minutes. Stand on
trays 5 minutes; transfer to wire rack to cool.

tip **For a firmer cookie, bake an extra 2 minutes.**

stained-glass christmas cookies

## STAINED-GLASS CHRISTMAS COOKIES

prep + cook time **45 minutes (+ refrigeration)**
makes **36**

250g butter, softened
2 teaspoons finely grated lemon rind
½ teaspoon almond essence
¾ cup (165g) caster sugar
1 egg
1 tablespoon water
2¼ cups (335g) plain flour
90g individually wrapped sugar-free
   fruit drops, assorted colours

**1** Preheat oven to 180°C/160°C fan-forced. Grease oven trays; line with baking paper.
**2** Beat butter, rind, essence, sugar, egg and the water in small bowl with electric mixer until smooth (do not overbeat). Transfer mixture to large bowl; stir in flour. Knead dough on floured surface until smooth; cover with plastic wrap, refrigerate 30 minutes.
**3** Meanwhile, using rolling pin, gently tap wrapped lollies to crush slightly. Unwrap lollies; separate by colour into small bowls.

**4** Roll dough between sheets of baking paper until 4mm thick. Cut shapes from dough using medium-sized cookie cutters; use very small cookie cutters to cut out the centre of each cookie. Place cookies on trays.
**5** Bake cookies about 5 minutes. Remove trays from oven; fill cut-out centre of each cookie with a different lolly colour. Return to oven 5 minutes. Cool cookies on oven trays.

## ALMOND JAM COOKIES

prep + cook time **40 minutes** makes **30**

185g butter, chopped
1 teaspoon vanilla extract
¾ cup (165g) caster sugar
2 egg yolks
½ cup (60g) almond meal
1½ cups (225g) plain flour
½ teaspoon baking power
2 tablespoons apricot jam, approximately
1 teaspoon grated lemon rind
2 tablespoons raspberry jam, approximately

**1** Preheat oven to 160°C/140°C fan-forced.
**2** Beat butter, extract, sugar and egg yolks in medium bowl with electric mixer until just combined. Stir in almond meal, flour and baking powder.
**3** Roll level tablespoons of mixture into balls; place on ungreased oven trays 5cm apart.
**4** Press a hollow into each ball about 1cm deep and 1.5cm wide using the handle of a lightly floured wooden spoon.
**5** Combine apricot jam with half of the rind. Combine raspberry jam with remaining rind. Carefully spoon a little apricot jam into half the cookies; spoon raspberry jam into remaining cookies.
**6** Bake cookies about 25 minutes; cool on trays.

tip **If jam sinks during cooking, top up with a little extra.**

almond jam cookies

honey jumbles

## HONEY JUMBLES

prep + cook time **40 minutes (+ cooling &
refrigeration)** makes **40**

60g butter
½ cup (110g) firmly packed brown sugar
¾ cup (270g) golden syrup
1 egg, beaten lightly
2½ cups (375g) plain flour
½ cup (75g) self-raising flour
½ teaspoon bicarbonate of soda
1 teaspoon ground cinnamon
½ teaspoon ground clove
2 teaspoons ground ginger
1 teaspoon mixed spice
icing
1 egg white
1½ cups (240g) icing sugar
2 teaspoons plain flour
1 tablespoon lemon juice, approximately
pink food colouring

**1** Preheat oven to 160°C/140°C fan-forced.
Grease oven trays.
**2** Stir butter, sugar and syrup in medium
saucepan over low heat until sugar dissolves;
cool 10 minutes.
**3** Transfer mixture to large bowl; stir in egg
and sifted dry ingredients, in two batches.
Knead dough on floured surface until dough
loses stickiness. Cover; refrigerate 30 minutes.
**4** Divide dough into 8 portions. Roll each
portion into 2cm-thick sausage; cut each
sausage into five 6cm lengths. Place about
3cm apart on oven trays; round ends with
lightly floured fingers, flatten slightly.
**5** Bake about 15 minutes; cool on trays.
**6** Meanwhile, make icing.
**7** Spread jumbles with pink and white icing.
**icing** Beat egg white lightly in small bowl;
gradually stir in sifted icing sugar and flour,
then enough juice to make icing spreadable.
Place half the mixture in another small bowl;
tint with colouring. Keep icings covered with
a damp tea towel while in use.

maple-syrup butter cookies

## MAPLE-SYRUP BUTTER COOKIES

prep + cook time **25 minutes** makes **24**

125g butter, softened
½ teaspoon vanilla extract
⅓ cup (80ml) maple syrup
¾ cup (110g) plain flour
¼ cup (35g) cornflour

**1** Preheat oven to 180°C/160°C fan-forced.
Grease oven trays; line with baking paper.
**2** Beat butter, extract and maple syrup in
small bowl with electric mixer until light and
fluffy; stir in combined sifted flours.
**3** Spoon mixture into piping bag fitted with
1cm fluted tube. Pipe stars about 3cm apart
onto trays.
**4** Bake cookies about 15 minutes; cool on trays.

choc-cherry bliss bombs

# CHOC-CHERRY BLISS BOMBS

prep + cook time **50 minutes (+ cooling)**  makes **280**

1⅓ cups (200g) milk chocolate Melts
60g butter
¼ cup (60ml) vegetable oil
⅓ cup (75g) caster sugar
2 eggs
1 cup (150g) self-raising flour
1 cup (150g) plain flour
3 x 55g Cherry Ripe bars, chopped finely
¼ cup (20g) desiccated coconut

**1** Stir chocolate, butter, oil and sugar in medium saucepan over low heat until smooth. Cool 15 minutes.
**2** Preheat oven to 180°C/160°C fan-forced. Grease oven trays; line with baking paper.
**3** Stir eggs and flours into chocolate mixture; stir in Cherry Ripe.
**4** Roll level ½ teaspoons of mixture into balls; roll half the balls in coconut. Place about 2cm apart on oven trays.
**5** Bake cookies about 10 minutes. Cool on trays. Serve in paper cones.

# HONEY, OAT & BARLEY HORSESHOES

prep + cook time **55 minutes**  makes **26**

125g butter, softened
½ cup (110g) caster sugar
1 egg
2 tablespoons golden syrup
2 tablespoons honey
½ cup (45g) rolled oats
½ cup (65g) rolled barley
2 cups (300g) plain flour
½ teaspoon bicarbonate of soda
1½ teaspoons cream of tartar
1 teaspoon ground ginger
1 teaspoon mixed spice
½ teaspoon ground clove
½ cup (45g) rolled oats, extra

**1** Preheat oven to 180°C/160°C fan-forced. Grease oven trays; line with baking paper.
**2** Beat butter, sugar and egg in small bowl with electric mixer until combined. Transfer to large bowl; stir in golden syrup, honey, oats, barley and sifted dry ingredients.
**3** Knead dough on floured surface until smooth. Sprinkle surface with extra rolled oats; roll level tablespoons of dough in oats into 12cm sausages. Shape into a horseshoe; place about 3cm apart on oven trays.
**4** Bake cookies about 20 minutes. Cool on wire racks.

honey, oat & barley horseshoes

peanut brittle cookies

## PEANUT BRITTLE COOKIES

prep + cook time **45 minutes (+ standing)** makes 42

125g butter, softened
¼ cup (70g) crunchy peanut butter
½ cup (100g) firmly packed brown sugar
1 egg
1½ cups (225g) plain flour
½ teaspoon bicarbonate of soda
peanut brittle
¾ cup (100g) roasted unsalted peanuts
½ cup (110g) caster sugar
2 tablespoons water

**1** Preheat oven to 160°C/140°C fan-forced.
Grease oven trays; line with baking paper.
**2** Make peanut brittle.
**3** Beat butter, peanut butter, sugar and egg in
small bowl with electric mixer until combined.
Stir in sifted dry ingredients and crushed
peanut brittle.
**4** Roll heaped teaspoons of mixture into balls
with floured hands. Place about 5cm apart
on oven trays; flatten slightly with hand.
**5** Bake cookies about 12 minutes. Cool on
trays.
**peanut brittle** Place nuts on baking-paper-
lined oven tray. Stir sugar and the water in
small frying pan, over heat, without boiling,
until sugar is dissolved. Bring to the boil; boil,
uncovered, without stirring, until golden brown.
Pour mixture over nuts; leave until set. Crush
coarsely in food processor.

polenta & orange biscuits

## POLENTA & ORANGE BISCUITS

prep + cook time **25 minutes** makes **30**

125g butter, softened
2 teaspoons finely grated orange rind
⅔ cup (110g) icing sugar
⅓ cup (55g) polenta
1 cup (150g) plain flour

**1** Preheat oven to 180°C/160°C fan-forced.
Grease oven trays; line with baking paper.
**2** Beat butter, rind and sifted icing sugar in
small bowl with electric mixer until just
combined; stir in polenta and sifted flour.
**3** Shape mixture into 30cm-rectangular log;
cut log into 1cm slices. Place slices on trays
2cm apart.
**4** Bake biscuits about 15 minutes. Stand on
trays 5 minutes; transfer to wire rack to cool.

chewy choc-chunk cookies

## CHEWY CHOC-CHUNK COOKIES

prep + cook time **30 minutes (+ refrigeration)**
makes **30**

2 eggs
1⅓ cups (295g) firmly packed brown sugar
1 teaspoon vanilla extract
1 cup (150g) plain flour
¾ cup (110g) self-raising flour
½ teaspoon bicarbonate of soda
½ cup (125ml) vegetable oil
1 cup (120g) coarsely chopped
    roasted pecans
¾ cup (120g) coarsely chopped raisins
1 cup (150g) dark chocolate Melts, halved
½ cup (95g) white Choc Bits

**1** Preheat oven to 200°C/180°C fan-forced. Grease oven trays.
**2** Beat eggs, sugar and extract in small bowl with electric mixer about 1 minute or until mixture changes to a paler colour.
**3** Stir in sifted dry ingredients then remaining ingredients (the mixture will be soft). Cover bowl; refrigerate 1 hour.
**4** Roll heaped tablespoons of mixture into balls; place on trays 6cm apart, flatten into 6cm rounds.
**5** Bake cookies about 10 minutes or until browned lightly. Stand on trays 5 minutes; transfer to wire racks to cool.

tip **You could use walnuts instead of pecans.**

## ALMOND CRISPS

prep + cook time **25 minutes**  makes **15**

125g butter, chopped
¼ cup (55g) caster sugar
1 cup (150g) self-raising flour
¼ cup (30g) almond meal
2 tablespoons flaked almonds

**1** Preheat oven to 200°C/180°C fan-forced. Grease oven trays.
**2** Beat butter and sugar in small bowl with electric mixer until smooth. Stir in flour and almond meal.
**3** Roll level tablespoons of mixture into balls; place onto trays 5cm apart. Flatten slightly with floured fork to 1cm thick; sprinkle with flaked almonds.
**4** Bake crisps about 10 minutes. Stand on trays 5 minutes; transfer to wire racks to cool.

almond crisps

wholemeal rosemary butter rounds

## CRUNCHY MUESLI COOKIES

prep + cook time **35 minutes**  makes **36**

1 cup (90g) rolled oats
1 cup (150g) plain flour
1 cup (220g) caster sugar
2 teaspoons ground cinnamon
¼ cup (35g) dried cranberries
⅓ cup (55g) finely chopped dried apricots
½ cup (70g) slivered almonds
125g butter
2 tablespoons golden syrup
½ teaspoon bicarbonate of soda
1 tablespoon boiling water

**1** Preheat oven to 150°C/130°C fan-forced. Grease oven trays; line with baking paper.
**2** Combine oats, flour, sugar, cinnamon, dried fruit and nuts in large bowl.
**3** Melt butter with golden syrup in small saucepan over low heat; add combined soda and the boiling water. Stir warm butter mixture into dry ingredients.
**4** Roll level tablespoons of mixture into balls, place on trays 5cm apart; flatten with hand.
**5** Bake cookies about 20 minutes. Cool cookies on trays.

crunchy muesli cookies

## WHOLEMEAL ROSEMARY BUTTER ROUNDS

prep + cook time **25 minutes**  makes **28**

125g butter, softened
2 teaspoons finely grated orange rind
1 cup (220g) firmly packed brown sugar
1⅓ cups (200g) wholemeal self-raising flour
1 cup (100g) roasted walnuts,
   chopped coarsely
⅔ cup (100g) raisins, halved
2 teaspoons dried rosemary
⅓ cup (80ml) orange juice
⅔ cup (50g) desiccated coconut
⅔cup (60g) rolled oats

**1** Preheat oven to 180°C/160°C fan-forced. Grease oven trays; line with baking paper.
**2** Beat butter, rind and sugar in small bowl with electric mixer until combined. Transfer to medium bowl; stir in flour then remaining ingredients.
**3** Roll rounded tablespoons of mixture into balls, place about 5cm apart on oven trays; flatten slightly.
**4** Bake cookies about 15 minutes. Cool on trays.

passionfruit butter biscuits

## WHITE CHOCOLATE MACADAMIA COOKIES

prep + cook time **25 minutes**  makes **24**

1½ cups (225g) plain flour
½ teaspoon bicarbonate of soda
¼ cup (55g) caster sugar
⅓ cup (75g) firmly packed brown sugar
125g butter, melted
½ teaspoon vanilla extract
1 egg
180g white eating chocolate,
    chopped coarsely
¾ cup (105g) roasted macadamias,
    chopped coarsely

**1** Preheat oven to 200°C/180°C fan-forced.
Grease two oven trays; line with baking paper.
**2** Sift flour, soda and sugars into large bowl.
Stir in butter, extract and egg, then chocolate
and nuts.
**3** Drop rounded tablespoons of mixture,
5cm apart on trays.
**4** Bake cookies about 10 minutes. Cool
on trays.

## PASSIONFRUIT BUTTER BISCUITS

prep + cook time **35 minutes (+ refrigeration)**
makes **40**

250g butter, softened
1⅓ cups (220g) icing sugar
2 cups (300g) plain flour
½ cup (75g) cornflour
⅓ cup (65g) rice flour
2 tablespoons passionfruit pulp

**1** Process butter, sugar and flours 2 minutes
or until mixture is combined. Add passionfruit;
process until mixture clings together.
**2** Transfer mixture to floured surface; knead
gently until smooth. Divide dough in half, roll
each half into 26cm log; wrap in plastic wrap.
Refrigerate 1 hour.
**3** Preheat oven to 160°C/140°C fan-forced.
Grease oven trays.
**4** Cut logs into 1cm slices; place slices on
trays 3cm apart.
**5** Bake biscuits about 20 minutes. Cool on
wire racks.

white chocolate macadamia cookies

coffee snaps

## COFFEE SNAPS

prep + cook time **30 minutes** makes **70**

125g butter, softened
1¼ cups (275g) firmly packed brown sugar
3 teaspoons ground coffee
½ teaspoon vanilla extract
1 egg
¾ cup (110g) plain flour
¾ cup (110g) self-raising flour
2 tablespoons (70g) coffee beans (70 beans)

**1** Preheat oven to 180°C/160°C fan-forced. Grease oven trays.
**2** Beat butter, sugar, coffee and extract in small bowl with electric mixer until pale and fluffy. Add egg; beat until just combined. Stir in sifted flours.
**3** Roll rounded teaspoons of mixture into balls; place on trays 3cm apart, top each with a coffee bean.
**4** Bake biscuits about 10 minutes or until browned. Stand on trays 5 minutes; transfer to wire rack to cool.

chocolate lace crisps

## CHOCOLATE LACE CRISPS

prep + cook time **35 minutes (+ refrigeration)** makes **24**

100g dark eating chocolate, chopped coarsely
80g butter, chopped
1 cup (220g) caster sugar
1 egg, beaten lightly
1 cup (150g) plain flour
2 tablespoons cocoa powder
¼ teaspoon bicarbonate of soda
¼ cup (40g) icing sugar

**1** Melt chocolate and butter in small saucepan over low heat. Transfer to medium bowl.
**2** Stir in caster sugar, egg and sifted flour, cocoa and soda. Cover; refrigerate 15 minutes or until mixture is firm enough to handle.
**3** Preheat oven to 180°C/160°C fan-forced. Grease oven trays; line with baking paper.
**4** Roll level tablespoons of mixture into balls; roll in icing sugar, place on trays 8cm apart.
**5** Bake crisps about 15 minutes; cool on trays.

anise-flavoured shortbread

## ANISE-FLAVOURED SHORTBREAD

prep + cook time 30 minutes (+ refrigeration)
makes 36

250g unsalted butter, softened
½ cup (80g) icing sugar
2 cups (300g) plain flour
½ cup (100g) rice flour
3 teaspoons ground aniseed

1 Beat butter and sifted icing sugar in medium bowl with electric mixer until light and fluffy. Add sifted flours and aniseed, in two batches, beating on low speed after each addition, only until combined.
2 Knead dough on floured surface until smooth. Cover; refrigerate 1 hour.
3 Preheat oven to 160°C/140°C fan-forced. Grease three oven trays.
4 Roll dough between sheets of baking paper until 5mm thick. Cut 36 x 6cm rounds from dough; place on oven trays about 3cm apart. Refrigerate 15 minutes.
5 Bake biscuits about 12 minutes. Cool on trays.

## PISTACHIO & CRANBERRY BISCOTTI

prep + cook time 1 hour 10 minutes (+ refrigeration & cooling) makes 60

60g unsalted butter, softened
1 teaspoon vanilla extract
1 cup (220g) caster sugar
2 eggs
1¾ cups (260g) plain flour
½ teaspoon bicarbonate of soda
¾ cup (110g) coarsely chopped
   roasted pistachios
1 cup (130g) dried cranberries
1 egg, extra
1 tablespoon water
2 tablespoons caster sugar, extra

1 Beat butter, extract and sugar in medium bowl until combined. Beat in eggs, one at a time. Stir in sifted flour and soda, then nuts and cranberries. Cover; refrigerate 1 hour.
2 Preheat oven to 180°C/160°C fan-forced. Grease oven tray.
3 Knead dough on floured surface until smooth but still sticky. Halve dough; shape each half into 30cm log. Place logs on tray.
4 Whisk extra egg with the water in small bowl. Brush egg mixture over logs; sprinkle with extra sugar.
5 Bake biscotti about 20 minutes or until firm. Cool 3 hours or overnight.
6 Preheat oven to 160°C/140°C fan-forced.
7 Using serrated knife, cut logs diagonally into 1cm slices. Place slices on ungreased oven trays.
8 Bake biscotti about 15 minutes or until dry and crisp, turning halfway through baking time. Cool on wire racks.

pistachio & cranberry biscotti

almond & chocolate florentines

## SNICKERDOODLES

prep + cook time **35 minutes (+ refrigeration)**
makes **50**

250g butter, softened
1 teaspoon vanilla extract
½ cup (110g) firmly packed brown sugar
1 cup (220g) caster sugar
2 eggs
2¾ cups (410g) plain flour
1 teaspoon bicarbonate of soda
½ teaspoon ground nutmeg
1 tablespoon caster sugar, extra
2 teaspoons ground cinnamon

**1** Beat butter, extract and sugars in small bowl with electric mixer until light and fluffy. Beat in eggs, one at a time, until just combined.
**2** Transfer mixture to large bowl; stir in combined sifted flour, soda and nutmeg, in two batches. Cover; refrigerate 30 minutes.
**3** Preheat oven to 180°C/160°C fan-forced.
**4** Combine extra caster sugar and cinnamon in small shallow bowl. Roll level tablespoons of dough into balls; roll balls in cinnamon sugar. Place on ungreased oven trays, 7cm apart.
**5** Bake snickerdoodles about 12 minutes. Cool on trays.

snickerdoodles

## ALMOND & CHOCOLATE FLORENTINES

prep + cook time **20 minutes (+ refrigeration)**
makes **28**

50g butter
¼ cup (55g) caster sugar
2 teaspoons honey
1 tablespoon plain flour
1 tablespoon cream
½ cup (40g) flaked almonds
50g dark cooking chocolate, melted

**1** Preheat oven to 200°C/180°C fan-forced. Grease four oven trays; line with baking paper.
**2** Bring butter, sugar, honey, flour and cream to the boil, stirring, in small saucepan. Reduce heat; cook, without stirring, 2 minutes. Remove from heat; stir in nuts.
**3** Drop level teaspoons of mixture about 8cm apart onto trays.
**4** Bake florentines about 6 minutes or until golden brown. Remove from oven; using metal spatula, push florentines into rounds. Cool on trays 1 minute then carefully lift onto baking-paper-lined wire rack to cool. Drizzle florentines with chocolate; refrigerate until set.

**ALLSPICE** also called pimento or jamaican pepper; tastes like a combination of nutmeg, cumin, clove and cinnamon. Available whole or ground.

**ALMONDS**

**blanched** brown skins removed.

**essence** made with almond oil and alcohol or another agent. *see essence/extract.*

**flaked** paper-thin slices.

**meal** also called ground almonds.

**slivered** small lengthways-cut pieces.

**BAKING POWDER** a raising agent consisting mainly of two parts cream of tartar to one part bicarbonate of soda (baking soda).

**BICARBONATE OF SODA** also known as baking soda.

**BRANDY** short for brandywine, the translation of the Dutch "brandwijn", burnt wine. A general term for a liqueur distilled from wine grapes (usually white). Cognac and Armagnac are two of the finest aged brandies available.

**BUTTER** use salted or unsalted ('sweet') butter; 125g is equal to 1 stick of butter.

**BUTTERMILK** in spite of its name, buttermilk is actually low in fat. Originally the term given to the slightly sour liquid left after butter was churned from cream, today it is intentionally made from no-fat or low-fat milk to which specific bacterial cultures have been added during the manufacturing process. It is readily available from the dairy department in supermarkets.

**CACHOUS** small, round cake-decorating sweets available in silver, gold and various colours.

**CARDAMOM** a spice native to India and used extensively in its cuisine; can be purchased in pod, seed or ground form. Has a distinctive aromatic, sweetly rich flavour and is one of the world's most expensive spices.

**CASHEWS** plump, kidney-shaped, golden-brown nuts having a distinctive sweet, buttery flavour and containing about 48 per cent fat. Because of this high fat content, they should be kept, sealed tightly, under refrigeration to avoid becoming rancid. Roasting cashews brings out their intense nutty flavour.

**CHERRY RIPE BARS** dark chocolate bar made from coconut and cherries; standard bar weighs 35g.

**CHOCOLATE**

**Choc Bits** also called chocolate chips and chocolate morsels. Hold their shape in baking and are ideal for decorating.

**dark eating** also called semi-sweet or luxury chocolate; made of a high percentage of cocoa liquor and cocoa butter, and little added sugar. Unless stated otherwise, we use dark eating chocolate as it's ideal for use in desserts and cakes.

**Melts** discs made of milk, white or dark compound chocolate; good for melting and moulding.

**milk** most popular eating chocolate, mild and very sweet; similar in make-up to dark with the difference being the addition of milk solids.

**white** contains no cocoa solids but derives its sweet flavour from cocoa butter. Very sensitive to heat.

**CHOCOLATE HAZELNUT SPREAD** also known as Nutella.

**CINNAMON** dried inner bark of the shoots of the cinnamon tree; comes in stick (quill) or ground form. It is one of the world's most common spices, used universally as a sweet, fragrant flavouring for both sweet and savoury foods.

**CLOVES** dried flower buds of a tropical tree; can be used whole or in ground form. They have a strong scent and taste so should be used sparingly.

**COCOA POWDER** also known as cocoa; dried, unsweetened, roasted ground cocoa beans.

**COCONUT**

**desiccated** unsweetened and concentrated, dried finely shredded.

**essence** synthetically produced from flavouring, oil and alcohol.

**flaked** dried flaked coconut flesh.

**shredded** thin strips of dried coconut flesh.

**COFFEE-FLAVOURED LIQUEUR** we used either Tia Maria or Kahlua.

**CORNFLAKES** breakfast cereal made of dehydrated then baked crisp flakes of corn.

**CORNFLOUR** also known as cornstarch. Available made from corn or wheat (wheaten cornflour, gluten-free, gives a lighter texture in cakes).

**CREAM** we use fresh pouring cream, also known as pure cream. It has no additives, and contains a minimum fat content of 35 per cent.

**thickened** a whipping cream that contains a thickener. Has a minimum fat content of 35 per cent.

**CREAM CHEESE** commonly known as Philadelphia or Philly, a soft cow-milk cheese with fat content of at least 33%.

# GLOSSARY

**CREAM OF TARTAR** the acid ingredient in baking powder; added to confectionery mixtures to help prevent sugar crystallising. Keeps frostings creamy and improves volume when beating egg whites.

**CUSTARD POWDER** instant mixture used to make pouring custard; similar to North American instant pudding mixes.

**CUMIN** also known as zeera or comino; resembling caraway in size, cumin is the dried seed of a plant related to the parsley family. Available dried as seeds or ground.

**DATES** fruit of the date palm tree, eaten fresh or dried, on their own or in prepared dishes. About 4cm to 6cm in length, oval and plump, thin-skinned, with a honey-sweet flavour and sticky texture.

**DRIED CRANBERRIES** dried sweetened cranberries; used in cooking sweet or savoury dishes. Can usually be substituted for or with other dried fruit in most recipes. Commercially labelled as craisins.

**DRIED CURRANTS** dried tiny, almost black raisins so-named from the grape type native to Corinth, Greece. These are not the same as fresh currants, which are the fruit of a plant in the gooseberry family.

**DRIED MIXED BERRIES** lightly crunchy dehydrated form of strawberries, blueberries, cherries. They can be eaten as is or used as an ingredient in cooking.

**EGGS** if a recipe calls for raw or barely cooked eggs, exercise caution if there is a salmonella problem in your area, particularly in food eaten by children and pregnant women.

**ESSENCE/EXTRACT** an essence is either a distilled concentration of a food quality or an artificial creation of it. Coconut and almond essences are synthetically produced substances used in small amounts to impart their respective flavours to foods. An extract is made by actually extracting the flavour from a food product. In the case of vanilla, pods are soaked, usually in alcohol, to capture the authentic flavour. Both extracts and essences will keep indefinitely if stored in a cool dark place.

**FLOUR**

**plain** also known as all-purpose; unbleached wheat flour is the best for baking: the gluten content ensures a strong dough, which produces a light result.

**rice** very fine, almost powdery, gluten-free flour; made from ground white rice. Used in baking, as a thickener, and in some Asian noodles and desserts.

**self-raising** plain (all purpose) flour sifted with baking powder in the proportion of 1 cup flour to 2 teaspoons baking powder.

**FOOD COLOURING** vegetable-based substances available in liquid, paste or gel form.

**GINGER**

**fresh** also called green or root ginger; the thick gnarled root of a tropical plant.

**ground** also called powdered ginger; used as a flavouring, it cannot be substituted for fresh.

**glacé** fresh ginger root preserved in sugar syrup; crystallised ginger (sweetened with cane sugar) can be substituted if rinsed with warm water and dried before using.

**GLACE CHERRIES** also known as candied cherries; boiled in heavy sugar syrup and then dried.

**GOLDEN SYRUP** a by-product of refined sugarcane; pure maple syrup or honey can be substituted. Golden syrup and treacle (a thicker, darker syrup not unlike molasses), also known as flavour syrups, are similar sugar products made by partly breaking down sugar into its component parts and adding water. Treacle is more viscous, and has a stronger flavour and aroma than golden syrup (which has been refined further and contains fewer impurities, so is lighter in colour and more fluid). Both can be used in baking and for making certain confectionery items.

**HAZELNUTS** also known as filberts; plump, grape-sized, rich, sweet nut having a brown skin that is removed by rubbing heated nuts together vigorously in a tea-towel.

**meal** is made by grounding the hazelnuts to a coarse flour texture for use in baking or as a thickener.

**HAZELNUT-FLAVOURED LIQUEUR** such as frangelico.

**HONEY** the variety sold in a squeezable container is not suitable for the recipes in this book.

**HUNDREDS AND THOUSANDS** tiny sugar-syrup-coated sugar crystals in various colours.

**JAM** also called preserve or conserve; a thickened mixture of a fruit and sugar. Usually eaten on toast for breakfast, it's also used as a filling or icing for biscuits and cakes.

**JELLY CRYSTALS** a combination of sugar, gelatine, colours and flavours; when dissolved in water, the solution sets as firm jelly.

**LEMON BUTTER** a commercial lemon curd or lemon-flavoured spread.

**MCADAMIAS** native to Australia; fairly large, slightly soft, buttery rich nut. Should always be stored in the fridge to prevent their high oil content turning them rancid.

**MAPLE-FLAVOURED SYRUP** is made from sugar cane and is also known as golden or pancake syrup. It is not an adequate substitute for pure maple syrup.

**MAPLE SYRUP** distilled from the sap of maple trees in Canada and parts of North America. Maple-flavoured syrup is not an adequate substitute for the real thing.

**MARZIPAN** a paste made from ground almonds, sugar and water. Similar to almond paste but sweeter, more pliable and finer in texture. Easily coloured and rolled into thin sheets to cover cakes, or sculpted into shapes for confectionery.

**MILK** unless stated otherwise, we use full-cream homogenised milk.

**MIXED PEEL** candied citrus peel.

**MIXED SPICE** a blend of ground spices usually consisting of cinnamon, allspice and nutmeg.

**MUESLI** also known as granola; a combination of grains (mainly oats), nuts and dried fruits. Some manufacturers toast their product in oil and honey, adding crispness and kilojoules.

**NUTMEG** a strong and pungent spice ground from the dried nut of an Indonesian native evergreen tree. Usually found ground but the flavour is more intense from a whole nut, available from spice shops, so it's best to grate your own. Found in mixed spice mixtures.

**OATBRAN** the hard and rather woody protective coating of oats which serves to protect the grain before it germinates.

**ORANGE-FLAVOURED LIQUEUR** brandy-based liqueur such as Grand Marnier or Cointreau.

**PEANUTS** also called groundnut, not in fact a nut but the pod of a legume. We mainly use unsalted roasted peanuts.

**PECANS** native to the US and now grown locally; pecans are golden brown, buttery and rich. Good in savoury as well as sweet dishes; walnuts are a good substitute.

**PISTACHIOS** green, delicately flavoured nuts inside hard off-white shells. Available salted or unsalted in their shells; you can also buy them shelled.

**POLENTA** also called cornmeal; a flour-like cereal made of dried corn (maize); also the name of the dish made from it.

**READY-MADE WHTIE ICING** also called prepared fondant; available in the baking section at supermarkets.

**ROLLED BARLEY** sliced barley kernels rolled flat into flakes. Like rolled oats, rolled barley is usually served as porridge.

**ROLLED OATS** flattened oat grain rolled into flakes and traditionally used for porridge. Instant oats are also available, but use traditional oats for baking.

**ROSEWATER** extract made from crushed rose petals, called gulab in India; used for its aromatic quality in many sweetmeats and desserts.

**SOUR CREAM** thick, commercially-cultured with a minimum fat content of 35 per cent.

**SUGAR**

**brown** an extremely soft, fine granulated sugar retaining molasses for its characteristic colour and flavour.

**caster** also known as superfine or finely granulated table sugar.

**icing** also called confectioners' sugar or powdered sugar; pulverised granulated sugar crushed together with a small amount (about 3 per cent) of cornflour.

**pure icing** also known as confectioners' sugar or powdered sugar.

**vanilla** granulated or caster sugar flavoured with a vanilla bean. Can be stored indefinitely.

**SUGAR-FREE FRUIT DROPS** individually wrapped fruit-flavoured hard lollies made with artificial sweetener.

**SWEETENED CONDENSED MILK** from which 60% of the water had been removed; the remaining milk is then sweetened with sugar.

**TOP 'N' FILL CARAMEL** a canned milk product made of condensed milk that has been boiled to a caramel.

**VANILLA**

**bean** dried long, thin pod from a tropical golden orchid grown in Central and South America and Tahiti. Tiny black seeds inside the bean are used to impart a vanilla flavour in baking and desserts.

**extract** distilled from the seeds of the vanilla pod.

**VEGETABLE OIL** any of a number of oils sourced from plants rather than animal fats.

**VIOLET CRUMBLE** a honeycomb bar coated in milk chocolate.

# CONVERSION CHART

## MEASURES

One Australian metric measuring cup holds approximately 250ml, one Australian metric tablespoon holds 20ml, one Australian metric teaspoon holds 5ml.

The difference between one country's measuring cups and another's is within a 2- or 3-teaspoon variance, and will not affect your cooking results. North America, New Zealand and the United Kingdom use a 15ml tablespoon. All cup and spoon measurements are level. The most accurate way of measuring dry ingredients is to weigh them. When measuring liquids, use a clear glass or plastic jug with metric markings.

We use large eggs with an average weight of 60g.

## DRY MEASURES

| METRIC | IMPERIAL |
|---|---|
| 15g | ½oz |
| 30g | 1oz |
| 60g | 2oz |
| 90g | 3oz |
| 125g | 4oz (¼lb) |
| 155g | 5oz |
| 185g | 6oz |
| 220g | 7oz |
| 250g | 8oz (½lb) |
| 280g | 9oz |
| 315g | 10oz |
| 345g | 11oz |
| 375g | 12oz (¾lb) |
| 410g | 13oz |
| 440g | 14oz |
| 470g | 15oz |
| 500g | 16oz (1lb) |
| 750g | 24oz (1½lb) |
| 1kg | 32oz (2lb) |

## LIQUID MEASURES

| METRIC | IMPERIAL |
|---|---|
| 30ml | 1 fluid oz |
| 60ml | 2 fluid oz |
| 100ml | 3 fluid oz |
| 125ml | 4 fluid oz |
| 150ml | 5 fluid oz (¼ pint/1 gill) |
| 190ml | 6 fluid oz |
| 250ml | 8 fluid oz |
| 300ml | 10 fluid oz (½ pint) |
| 500ml | 16 fluid oz |
| 600ml | 20 fluid oz (1 pint) |
| 1000ml (1 litre) | 1¾ pints |

## LENGTH MEASURES

| METRIC | IMPERIAL |
|---|---|
| 3mm | ⅛in |
| 6mm | ¼in |
| 1cm | ½in |
| 2cm | ¾in |
| 2.5cm | 1in |
| 5cm | 2in |
| 6cm | 2½in |
| 8cm | 3in |
| 10cm | 4in |
| 13cm | 5in |
| 15cm | 6in |
| 18cm | 7in |
| 20cm | 8in |
| 23cm | 9in |
| 25cm | 10in |
| 28cm | 11in |
| 30cm | 12in (1ft) |

## OVEN TEMPERATURES

These oven temperatures are only a guide for conventional ovens.
For fan-forced ovens, check the manufacturer's manual.

| | °C (CELSIUS) | °F (FAHRENHEIT) | GAS MARK |
|---|---|---|---|
| Very slow | 120 | 250 | ½ |
| Slow | 150 | 275-300 | 1-2 |
| Moderately slow | 160 | 325 | 3 |
| Moderate | 180 | 350-375 | 4-5 |
| Moderately hot | 200 | 400 | 6 |
| Hot | 220 | 425-450 | 7-8 |
| Very hot | 240 | 475 | 9 |

# INDEX

First published in 2009 by ACP Books, Sydney.
Reprinted 2010.
ACP Books are published by ACP Magazines Pty Limited.

ACP BOOKS

**General manager** Christine Whiston
**Editor-in-chief** Susan Tomnay
**Creative director** Hieu Chi Nguyen
**Art director** Hannah Blackmore
**Senior editor** Stephanie Kistner
**Designer** Clare O'Loughlin
**Recipe compiler** Abby Pfahl
**Food director** Pamela Clark
**Home economist** Nicole Jennings
**Sales & rights director** Brian Cearnes
**Marketing manager** Bridget Cody
**Senior business analyst** Rebecca Varela
**Circulation manager** Jama Mclean
**Operations manager** David Scotto
**Production manager** Victoria Jefferys

**Published by** ACP Books, a division of ACP Magazines Ltd,
54 Park St, Sydney; GPO Box 4088, Sydney, NSW 2001.
phone (02) 9282 8618; fax (02) 9267 9438.
acpbooks@acpmagazines.com.au; www.acpbooks.com.au

**Printed by** Toppan Printing Co., China.

**Australia** Distributed by Network Services, phone +61 2 9282 8777;
fax +61 2 9264 3278; networkweb@networkservicescompany.com.au
**United Kingdom** Distributed by Australian Consolidated Press (UK),
phone (01604) 642 200; fax (01604) 642 300; books@acpuk.com
**New Zealand** Distributed by Netlink Distribution Company, phone (9) 366 9966; ask@ndc.co.nz
**South Africa** Distributed by PSD Promotions,
phone (27 11) 392 6065/6/7; fax (27 11) 392 6079/80; orders@psdprom.co.za
**Canada** Distributed by Publishers Group Canada
phone (800) 663 5714; fax (800) 565 3770; service@raincoast.com

A catalogue record for this book is available from the National Library of Australia.

ISBN: 978-1-86396-983-3

© ACP Magazines Ltd 2009
ABN 18 053 273 546

**Cover** White chocolate mud cakes, page 24
**Photographer** Ben Dearnley
**Stylist** Marie-Helene Clauzon

**Send recipe enquiries to:**
recipeenquiries@acpmagazines.com.au